SPECTRUM®
EARLY YEARS

Basic Beginnings
FUNDAMENTAL
SKILLS

Published by Spectrum®
an imprint of Carson-Dellosa Publishing LLC
Greensboro, NC

Spectrum
An imprint of Carson-Dellosa Publishing, LLC
P.O. Box 35665
Greensboro, NC 27425-5665

carsondellosa.com

ISBN 978-1-60996-891-5   01-044127784

Table of Contents

Welcome to *Basic Beginnings*

Basic Beginnings is a creative and developmentally appropriate series designed to fuel your child's learning potential. The early years of your child's life are bursting with cognitive and physical development. Therefore, it is essential to prepare your child for the basic skills and fine motor skills that are emphasized in the 21st century classroom. Basic skills include concepts such as recognizing letters, numbers, colors, shapes, and identifying same, different, and sequences of events. Fine motor skills are movements produced by small muscles or muscle groups, such as the precise hand movements required to write, cut, glue, and color. A child in preschool spends a lot of his or her day developing these muscles.

Basic Beginnings approaches learning through a developmentally appropriate process—ensuring your child is building the best foundation possible for preschool. Each activity is unique and fun, and stimulates your child's fine motor skills, hand-eye coordination, and ability to follow directions. Help your child complete the activities in this book. Each activity includes simple, step-by-step instructions. Provide your child with pencils, crayons, scissors, and glue for the various and creative activities he or she is about to discover.

Each book also includes three cutout mini books that reinforce the concepts your child is learning. You and your child will enjoy reading these simple stories together. Your child can make each story his or her own by coloring it, cutting it out, and, with your help, stapling the story together. Allow him or her to share the stories with you and others. Your child will begin to recognize sight words, hear vowel sounds, and understand sequences of events as he or she shares these delightful stories. With *Basic Beginnings*, the learning is never confined to the pages!

Introduction to *Fundamental Skills*

Fundamental Skills provides you with everything you need to help develop and build a solid educational foundation for your young learner. This engaging resource is a wealth of easy and fun activities that cover important topics such as: letter and sound recognition, identifying colors, tracing and drawing shapes, and recognizing and counting numbers. You will quickly discover that the activities in *Fundamental Skills* were not only designed to teach, but also to delight and motivate your child to want to learn!

Each activity includes simple directions for your child. Carefully read the directions to your child. Give your child time to complete the activity in his or her own creative way, providing guidance when necessary. In this workbook, your child will practice tracing letters, shapes, and numbers with a pencil or crayon. If your child struggles with holding a pencil correctly or mastering more difficult writing strokes, allow your child to practice drawing straight, curved, and circular lines freely on a sheet of paper. Remember, your child is at the beginning of his or her writing readiness and with time and practice he or she will be able to write all the letters, shapes, and numbers in this book.

Before beginnings activities in this workbook, try some of the fun, hands-on learning ideas below to introduce your child to letters, colors, shapes, and numbers.

Tactile Flashcards

Cut out letters of the alphabet from sandpaper, felt, or other textured paper. Glue the letters to small sheets of paper to create tactile flashcards. Give your child one card at a time and have him or her feel the letter and then say it out loud.

Thumbprint Rainbow

Give your child a large sheet of paper and finger paint or water-based paint of different colors. Encourage your child to use his or her thumb to make thumbprints on the paper. Help your child arrange the colored thumbprints to make a rainbow pattern.

Bend-a-Shape

Give your child several pieces of cooled, cooked spaghetti of varying lengths. Have your child work at a flat surface. Encourage him or her to bend and move the spaghetti to make different shapes. You can also give your child pieces of yarn.

Dot-to-Dot Numbers

Use a series of dots to write the different numbers 1 to 10. Have your child connect the dots to create the numbers. Ask your child to tell you which number he or she just created by connecting the dots.

The Letter Aa

Directions: Trace uppercase **A**. Trace lowercase **a**.

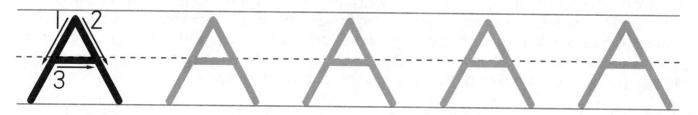

Directions: Color the pictures that start with the letter **Aa**.

Directions: Circle each uppercase **A** and lowercase **a**.

A a d V a X A

a b p A N a A

Fundamental Skills

The Letter Bb

Directions: Trace uppercase **B**. Trace lowercase **b**.

B B B B B B B

b b b b b b b b

Directions: Find and color the things that start with the letter **Bb**.

7

Fundamental Skills

The Letter Cc

Directions: Trace uppercase **C**. Trace lowercase **c**.

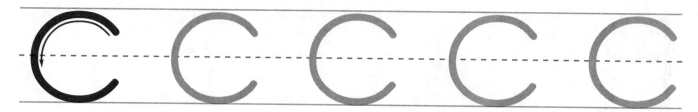

Directions: Circle the pictures that start with the letter **Cc**.

Directions: Circle each uppercase **C** and lowercase **c**.

C Q c C o c o

e c C D c C A

The Letter Dd

Directions: Trace uppercase **D**. Trace lowercase **d**.

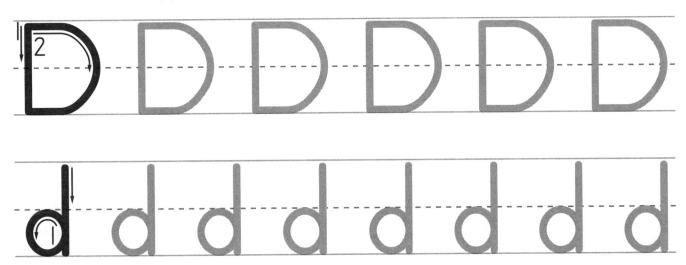

Directions: Find and color the things that start with the letter **Dd**.

9

Fundamental Skills

The Letter Ee

Directions: Trace uppercase **E**. Trace lowercase **e**.

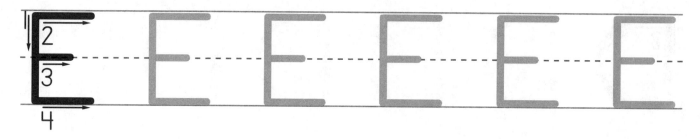

Directions: Point to the pictures that start with the letter **Ee**.

Directions: Circle each uppercase **E** and lowercase **e**.

F   E   e   F   F   e   E   A

e   f   F   E   E   K   a   e

The Letter Ff

Directions: Trace uppercase **F**. Trace lowercase **f**.

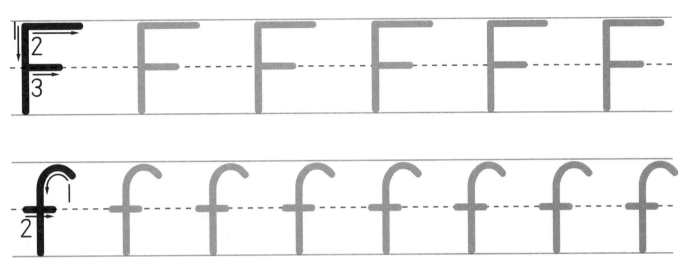

Directions: Find and color the things that start with the letter **Ff**.

Fundamental Skills

The Letter Gg

Directions: Trace uppercase **G**. Trace lowercase **g**.

G G G G G G

g g g g g g g g g

Directions: Color the pictures that start with the letter **Gg** green.

Directions: Circle each uppercase **G** and lowercase **g**.

p   G   p   g   a   G   g

g   b   G   g   Q   O   G

2

Little ant had a map.

4

He ran and ran and ran.

Ant and the Map

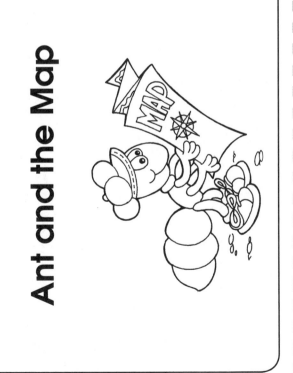

1

Ant had to follow the path.

3

13

6

Ant had to go back to the path.

8

Notes to Parents

Directions: First, ask your child to color the mini book. Then, help him or her cut along the dotted lines. Next, have your child arrange the pages in the correct order. Staple the pages together. Read the story out loud to your child.

Extension ideas:
1. Read the list of short **Aa** words that appear in the story: **ant, ants, and, back, apples, had, can, path, map, ran, last, sat.**
2. Have your child circle each uppercase **A** and lowercase **a**.
3. Help your child make his or her own map. Hide a treasure for your child and help him or her use the map to find it.

5

Ant sat down. Can he last?

7

Look! Many ants are eating apples.

The Letter Hh

Directions: Trace uppercase **H**. Trace lowercase **h**.

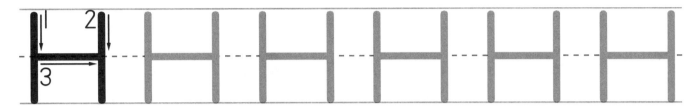

Directions: Draw an **X** on the pictures that start with the letter **Hh**.

Directions: Circle each uppercase **H** and lowercase **h**.

A   H   h   H   h   N   H

h   h   b   n   A   N   H   h

17

The Letter Ii

Directions: Trace uppercase **I**. Trace lowercase **i**.

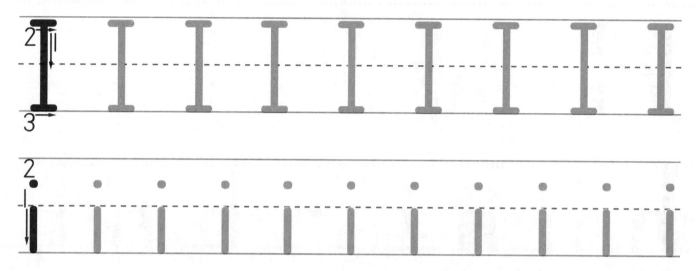

Directions: Circle the pictures that start with the letter **Ii**.

Directions: Circle each uppercase **I** and lowercase **i**.

L I T I i L T

T i I i I i I

Fundamental Skills

The Letter Jj

Directions: Trace uppercase **J**. Trace lowercase **j**.

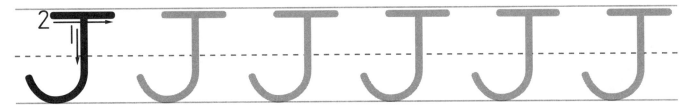

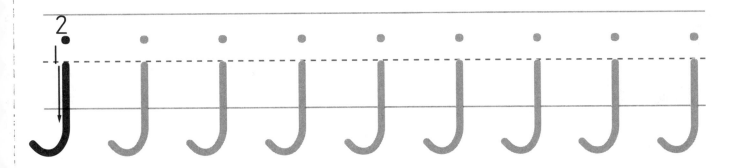

Directions: Find and color the things that start with the letter **Jj**.

Fundamental Skills

The Letter Kk

Directions: Trace uppercase **K**. Trace lowercase **k**.

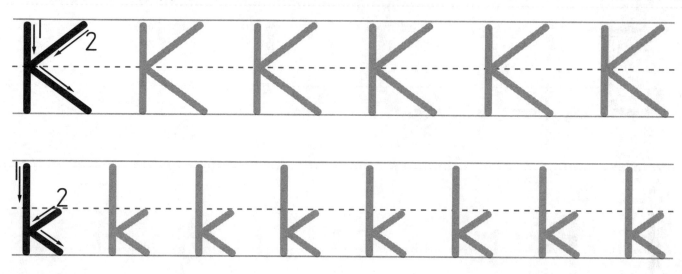

Directions: Color the pictures that start with the letter **Kk**.

Directions: Circle each uppercase **K** and lowercase **k**.

K k X K k X K

v K k A x V k

Fundamental Skills

The Letter Ll

Directions: Trace uppercase **L**. Trace lowercase **l**.

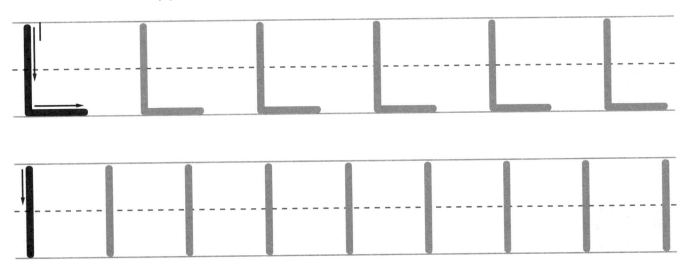

Directions: Find and color the things that start with the letter **Ll**.

21

The Letter Mm

Directions: Trace uppercase **M**. Trace lowercase **m**.

Directions: Point to the pictures that start with the letter **Mm**.

Directions: Circle each uppercase **M** and lowercase **m**.

M m X M M X m

n m M w N m n

22

The Letter Nn

Directions: Trace uppercase **N**. Trace lowercase **n**.

Directions: Find and color the things that start with the letter **Nn**.

Fundamental Skills

The Letter Oo

Directions: Trace uppercase **O**. Trace lowercase **o**.

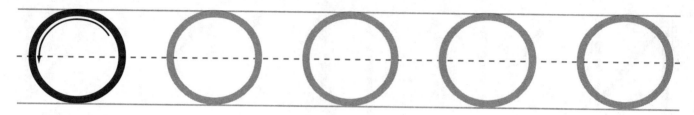

Directions: Color the pictures that start with the letter **Oo**.

Directions: Circle each uppercase **O** and lowercase **o**.

Q   o   O   O   a   G   o

a   o   o   Q   o   q

Fundamental Skills

The Letter Pp

Directions: Trace uppercase **P**. Trace lowercase **p**.

P P P P P P P

p p p p p p p p

Directions: Find and color the things that start with the letter **Pp**.

Fundamental Skills

The Letter Qq

Directions: Trace uppercase **Q**. Trace lowercase **q**

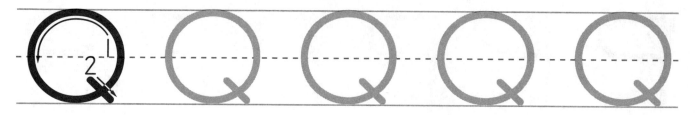

Directions: Draw an **X** on the pictures that start with the letter **Qq**

Directions: Circle each uppercase **Q** and lowercase **q**

O   Q   q   G   a   q   G

a   b   Q   D   Q   q   Q

26

The Letter Rr

Directions: Trace uppercase **R**. Trace lowercase **r**.

R R R R R R R

r r r r r r r r r

Directions: Find and color the things that start with the letter **Rr**.

27

Fundamental Skills

The Letter Ss

Directions: Trace uppercase **S**. Trace lowercase **s**.

S S S S S S

S S S S S S S S

Directions: Circle the pictures that start with the letter **Ss**.

Directions: Circle each uppercase **S** and lowercase **s**.

Z   S   Z   S   X   s   s

K   s   S   S   N   S   x

Fundamental Skills

The Letter Tt

Directions: Trace uppercase **T**. Trace lowercase **t**.

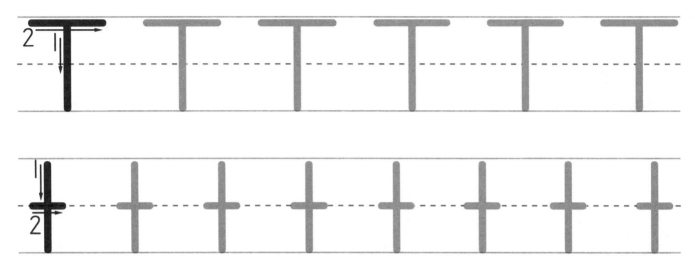

Directions: Find and color the things that start with the letter **Tt**.

The Letter Uu

Directions: Trace uppercase **U**. Trace lowercase **u**.

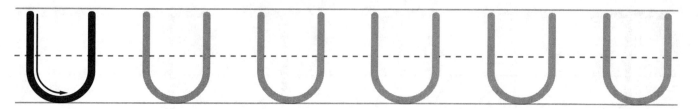

Directions: Color the pictures that start with the letter **Uu**.

Directions: Circle each uppercase **U** and lowercase **u**.

u U n U W u W

u U V V U u X

30   *Fundamental Skills*

The Letter Vv

Directions: Trace uppercase **V**. Trace lowercase **v**.

Directions: Find and color the things that start with the letter **Vv**.

Fundamental Skills

The Letter Ww

Directions: Trace uppercase **W**. Trace lowercase **w**.

Directions: Point to the pictures that start with the letter **Ww**.

Directions: Circle each uppercase **W** and lowercase **w**.

X   W   Z   V   w   X   w

w   w   W   W   N   W   Z

32

Fundamental Skills

The Letter Xx

Directions: Trace uppercase **X**. Trace lowercase **x**.

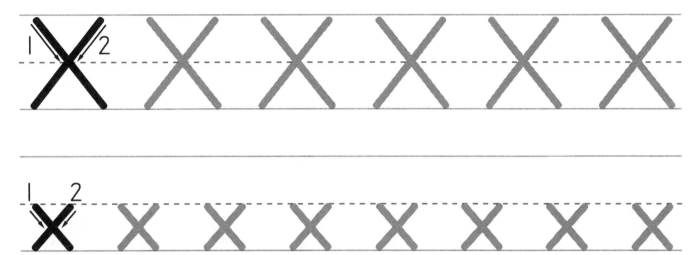

Directions: Find and color the things that have the letter **Xx** in them.

Fundamental Skills

The Letter Yy

Directions: Trace uppercase **Y**. Trace lowercase **y**.

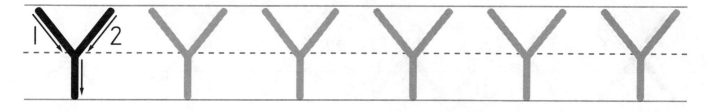

Directions: Color the pictures that start with the letter **Yy**.

Directions: Circle each uppercase **Y** and lowercase **y**.

y Y v V x Y Y

W y Y y N X y

34

Fundamental Skills

The Letter Zz

Directions: Trace uppercase **Z**. Trace lowercase **z**.

Z Z Z Z Z Z Z Z

z z z z z z z z z z z z

Directions: Find and color the things that start with the letter **Zz**.

35

Fundamental Skills

Uppercase Dot-to-Dot

Directions: Connect the dots from **A** to **Z**. Color the surprise.

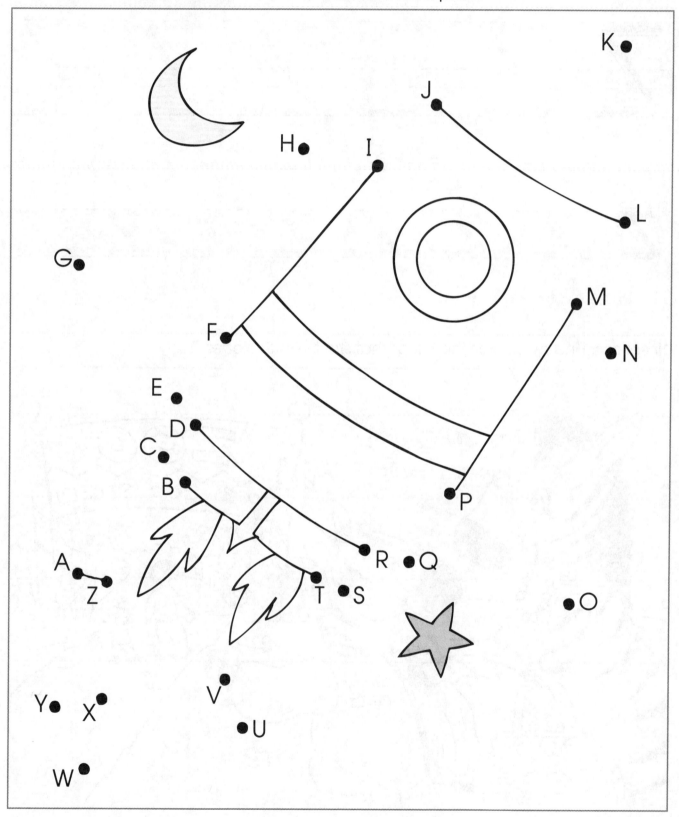

Fundamental Skills

2

Joe lost his bone.

4

The bone is not by the soap.

**Oh No!
Joe's
Bone**

1

3

Use your nose!

6

The bone is not by the rose.

8

Notes to Parents

Directions: First, ask your child to color the mini book. Then, help him or her cut along the dotted lines. Next, have your child arrange the pages in the correct order. Staple the pages together. Read the story out loud to your child.

Extension ideas:

1. Have your child circle each uppercase **O** and lowercase **o** with a crayon.

2. Read the list of long **Oo** words that appear in the story: **oh, no, Joe, bone, nose, soap, boat, rose, cone.**

3. Draw an oval. Brush the inside of the oval with glue. Place cereal or other dry food on the glue to make a mosaic.

5

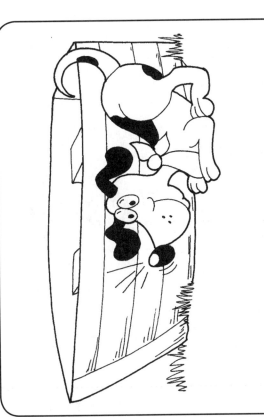

The bone is not by the boat.

7

The bone is in the cone.

Practice Printing the Alphabet

Directions: Trace the letters.

Circles and Squares

Directions: Trace the circle with a **red** crayon.

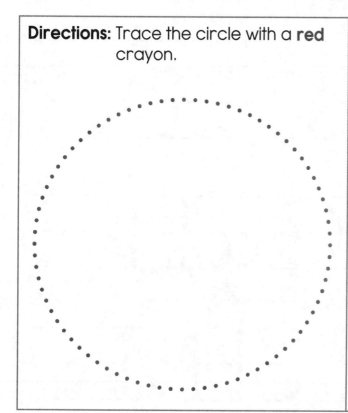

Directions: Draw an **X** on each circle.

Directions: Trace the square with a **blue** crayon.

Directions: Color the square frame. Draw a picture of yourself in the frame.

Fundamental Skills

Triangles and Rectangles

Directions: Trace the triangle with a green crayon.

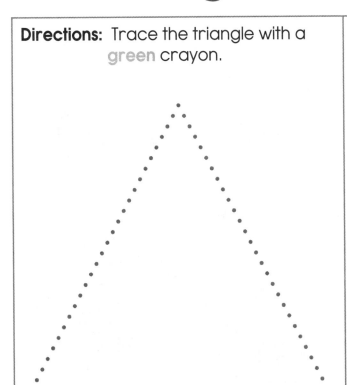

Directions: Color each picture that is the same shape as a triangle.

Directions: Trace the rectangle with your favorite color.

Directions: Color the rectangles yellow.

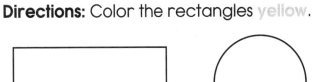

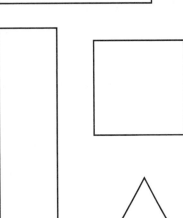 

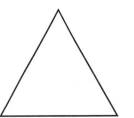 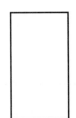

43

Stars and Rhombuses

Directions: Trace the star with a **purple** crayon.

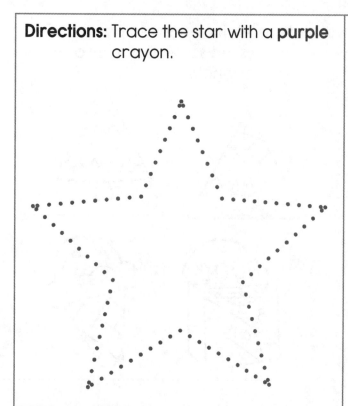

Directions: Draw an **X** on each star.

Directions: Trace the rhombus with a **pink** crayon.

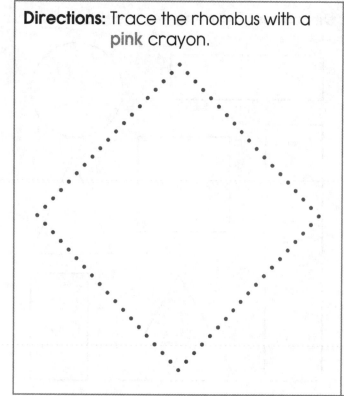

Directions: Color each picture that is the same shape as a rhombus.

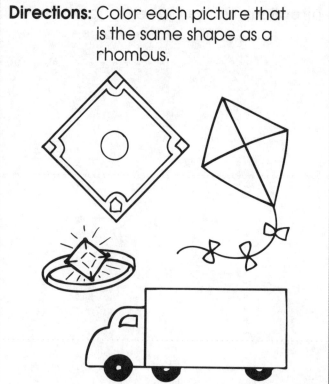

Ovals and Octagons

Directions: Trace the oval with a **gray** crayon.

Directions: Draw an **X** on each oval.

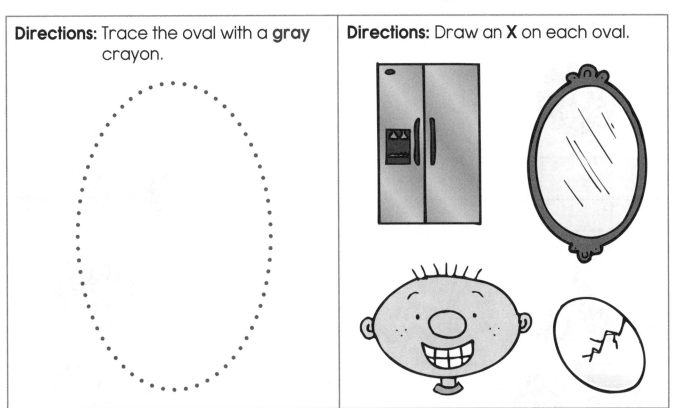

Directions: Trace the octagon with an **orange** crayon.

Directions: Color the octagons **red**.

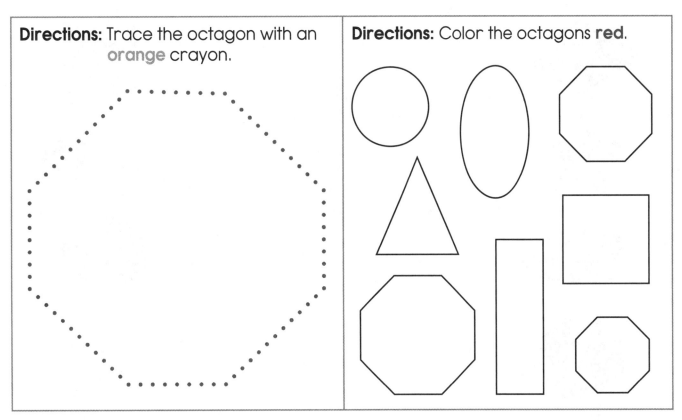

Match the Shapes!

Directions: Draw lines to match the shapes that are the same.

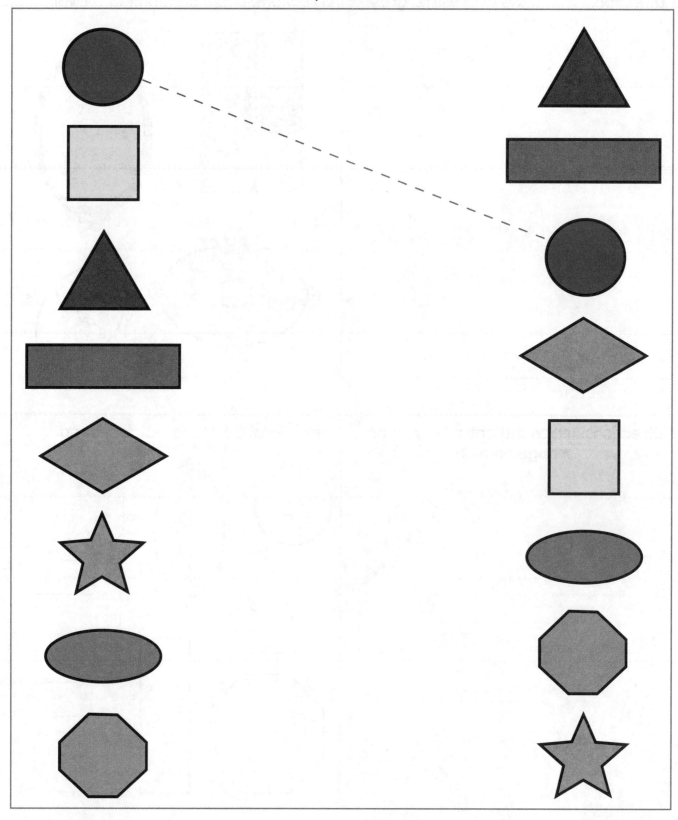

46

Finish the Shapes

Directions: Draw the other half. Then, color.

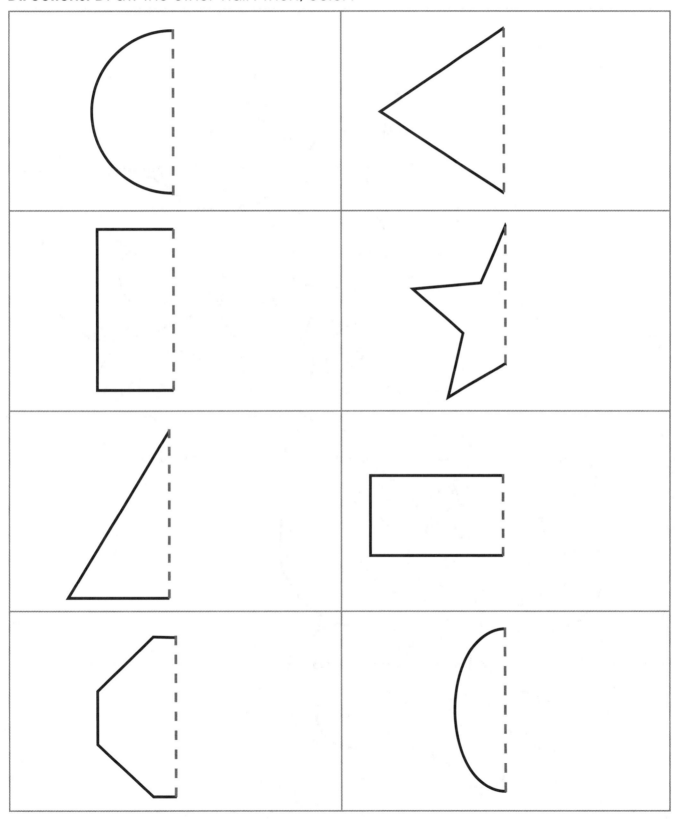

Butterfly Fun

Directions: Read the color words. Color the butterflies.

The Number 0

Directions: Count the fish. Draw **0** fish.

Directions: Trace the number **0**. Trace the word **zero**.

0 0 0 0 0 0 0

zero zero zero

Directions: Draw **0** cookies on the plate.

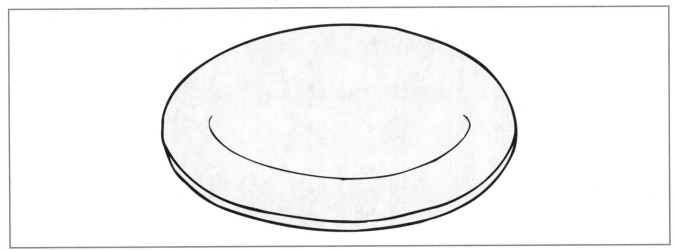

49

The Number 1

Directions: Color 1 puppy.

Directions: Trace the number 1. Trace the word **one**.

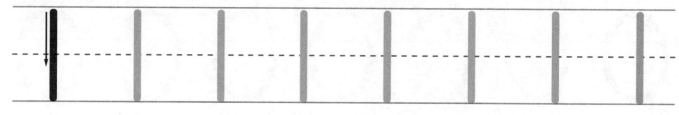

Directions: Connect the dots. What number did you make?

Fundamental Skills

The Number 2

Directions: Color **2** gorillas.

Directions: Trace the number **2**. Trace the word **two**.

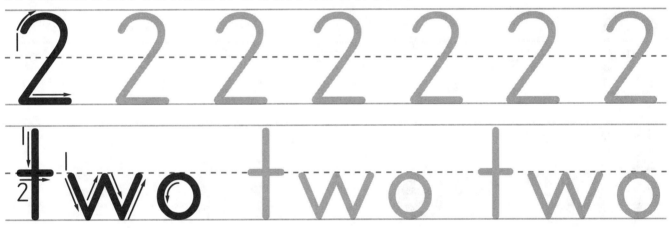

Directions: Connect the dots. Draw another cake.

The Number 3

Directions: Count **3** ice cream cones. Draw a cherry on each.

Directions: Trace the number **3**. Trace the word **three**.

3 3 3 3 3 3 3

three three

Directions: Connect the dots. Color.

Fundamental Skills

The Number 4

Directions: Color **4** ants.

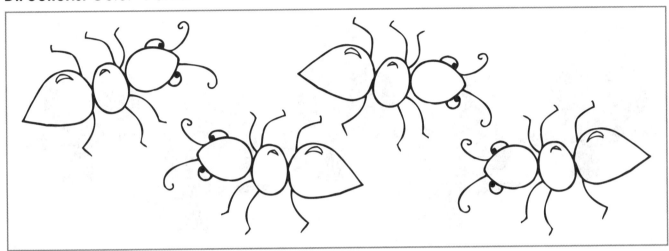

Directions: Trace the number **4**. Trace the word **four**.

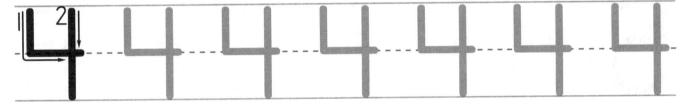

Directions: Draw **4** apples on the tree.

Fundamental Skills

The Number 5

Directions: Count **5** owls. Hoot like an owl **5** times.

Directions: Trace the number **5**. Trace the word **five**.

5 5 5 5 5 5 5 5

five five five

Directions: Connect the dots. Color.

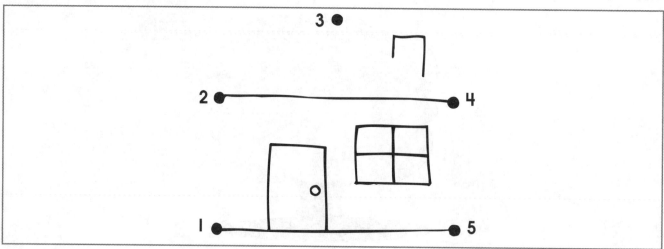

54

2

Five mice like to ride bikes.

4

Five mice like to glide.

1

Five Mice

3

Five mice like to hike.

55

6

Five mice like to slide.

8

Notes to Parents

Directions: First, ask your child to color the mini book. Then, help him or her cut along the dotted lines. Next, have your child arrange the pages in the correct order. Staple the pages together. Read the story out loud to your child.

Extension ideas:
1. Read the list of long **Ii** words that appear in the story: **five, mice, like, ride, bikes, hike, slide, glide, climb, line.**
2. Ask your child to count the mice on each page of the mini book. Have him or her jump up and down each time he or she counts a mouse.
3. Make a construction paper ice cream cone. Glue a picture of something that has a long Ii sound on each scoop of ice cream.

5

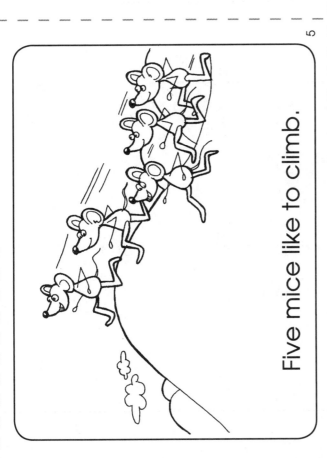

Five mice like to climb.

7

Five mice run to the finish line.

The Number 6

Directions: Count **6** carrots. Draw a bunny.

Directions: Trace the number **6**. Trace the word **six**.

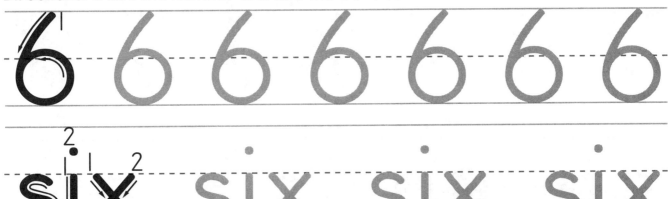

Directions: Draw **6** balls.

The Number 7

Directions: Color **7** parrots.

Directions: Trace the number **7**. Trace the word **seven**.

7 7 7 7 7 7 7

seven seven

Directions: Connect the dots.

Fundamental Skills

The Number 8

Directions: Color **8** rockets.

Directions: Trace the number **8**. Trace the word **eight**.

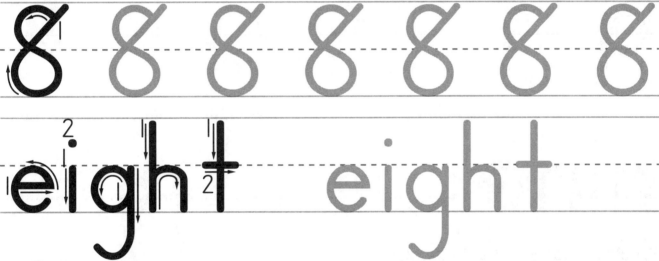

Directions: Draw **8** stars.

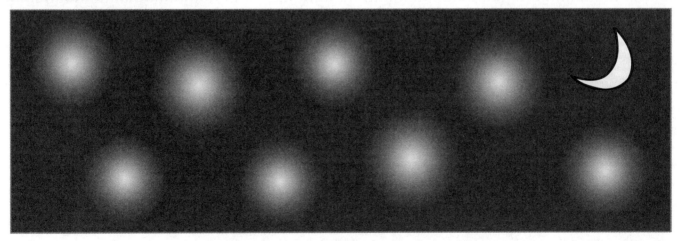

Fundamental Skills

The Number 9

Directions: Count **9** umbrellas. Draw rain.

Directions: Trace the number **9**. Trace the word **nine**.

9 9 9 9 9 9 9 9 9

nine nine nine

Directions: Connect the dots. Color.

Fundamental Skills

The Number 10

Directions: Color **10** raccoons.

Directions: Trace the number **10**. Trace the word **ten**.

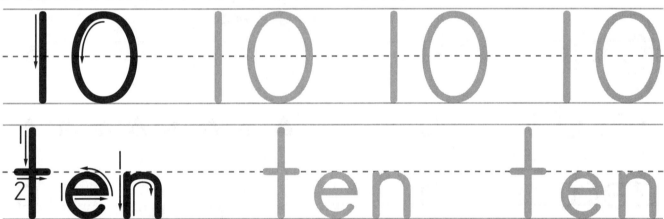

Directions: Connect the dots. Color the surprise.

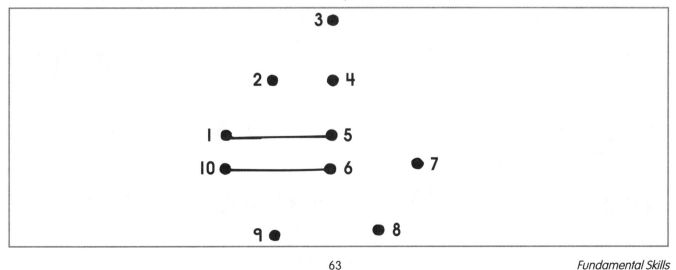

Fundamental Skills

Review 0 to 10

Directions: Match the number word, to the numeral, and then to the set of objects. The first one is done for you.

six	0	
seven	1	◆ ◆ ◆ ◆
two	2	❖ ❖ ❖ ❖ ❖
one	3	✳ ✳ ✳ ✳ ✳ ✳ ✳ ✳ ✳
four	4	▼
three	5	▲ ▲ ▲ ▲ ▲ ▲ ▲ ▲
zero	6	▢ ▢
nine	7	✿ ✿ ✿ ✿ ✿
five	8	▢ ▢ ▢
eight	9	▼ ▼ ▼ ▼ ▼ ▼
ten	10	✳ ✳ ✳ ✳ ✳ ✳ ✳ ✳ ✳ ✳

Fundamental Skills